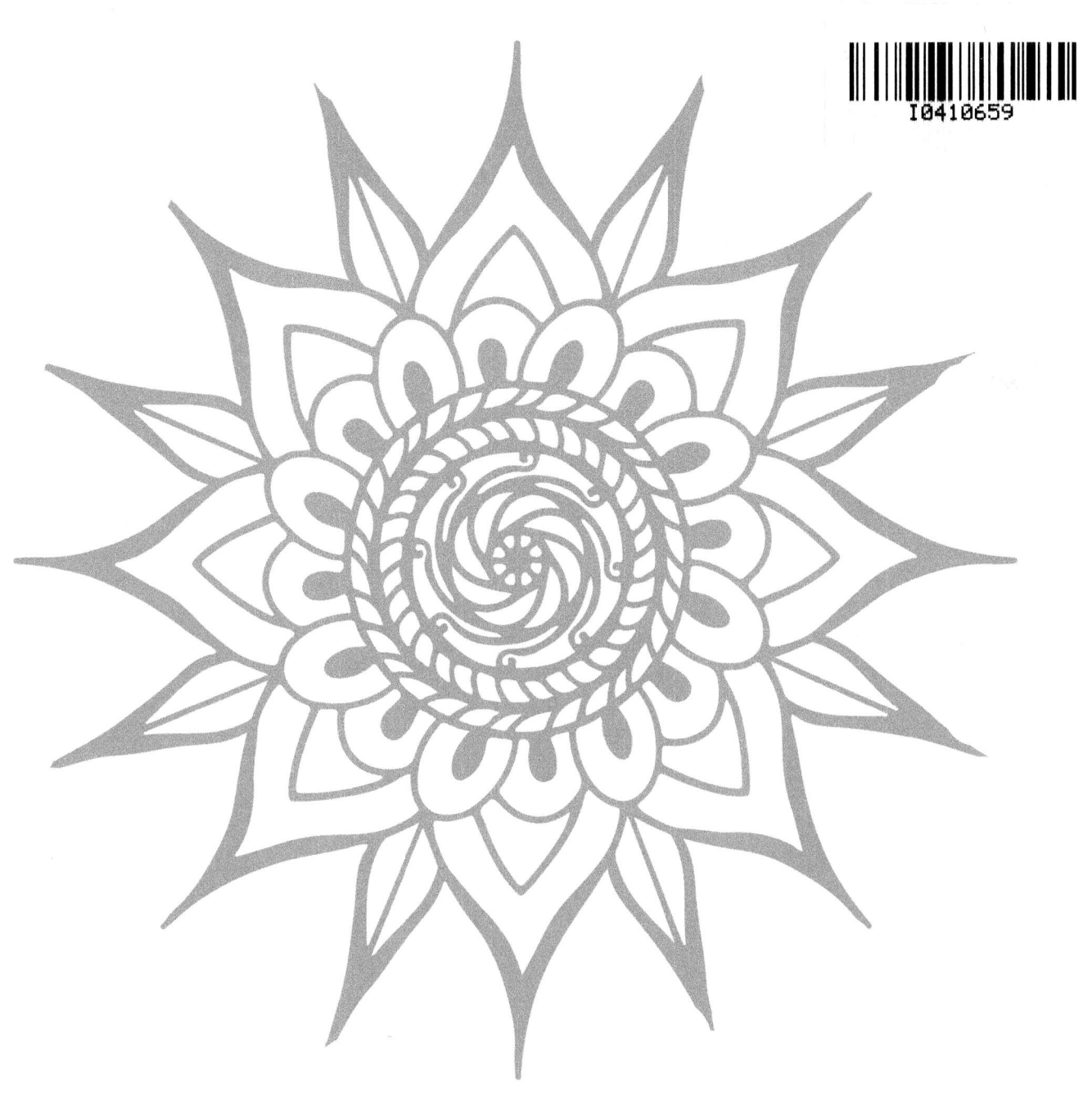

"Peace comes from within.
Do not seek it without."

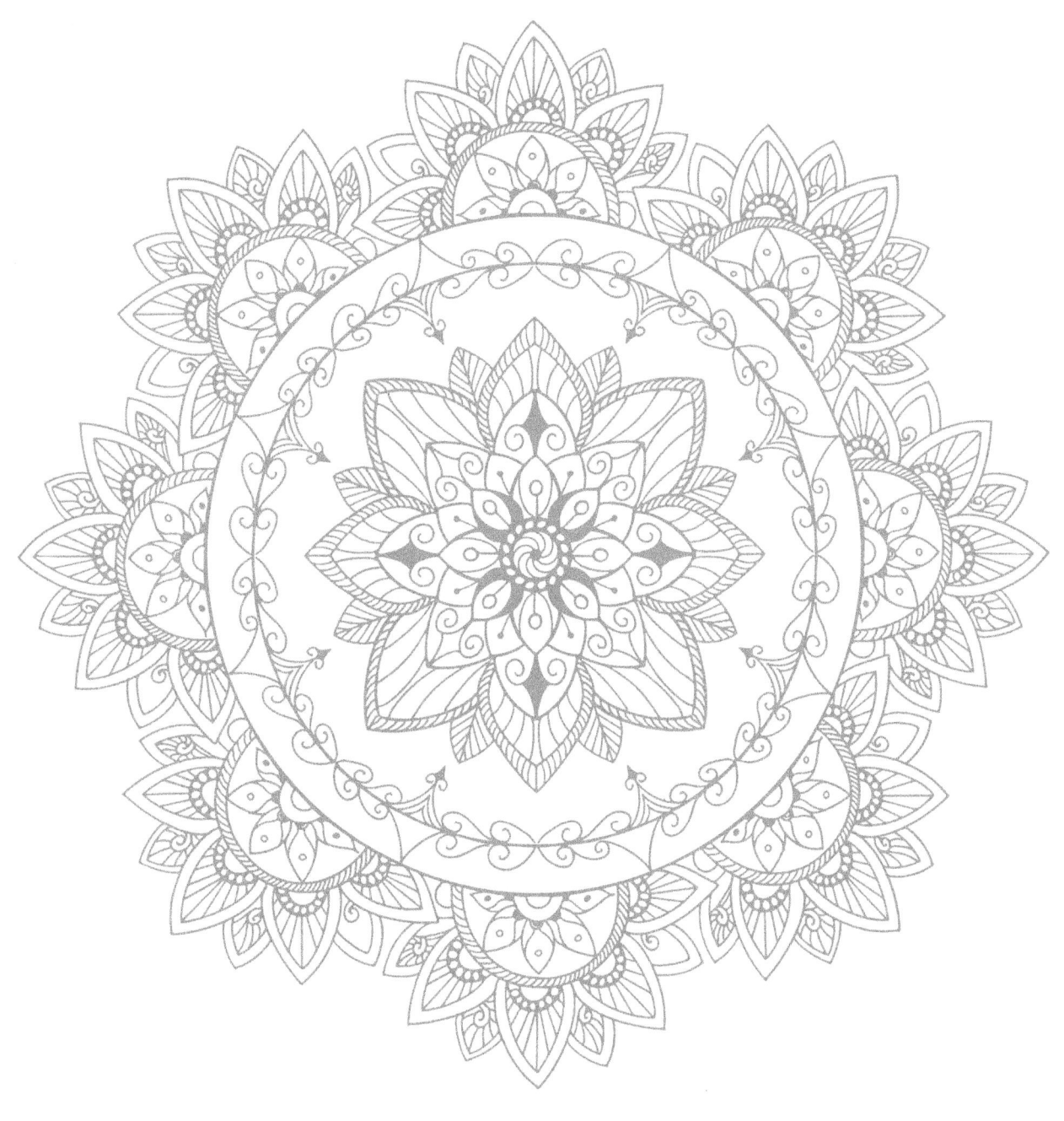

"In the midst of movement and chaos,
keep stillness inside of you."

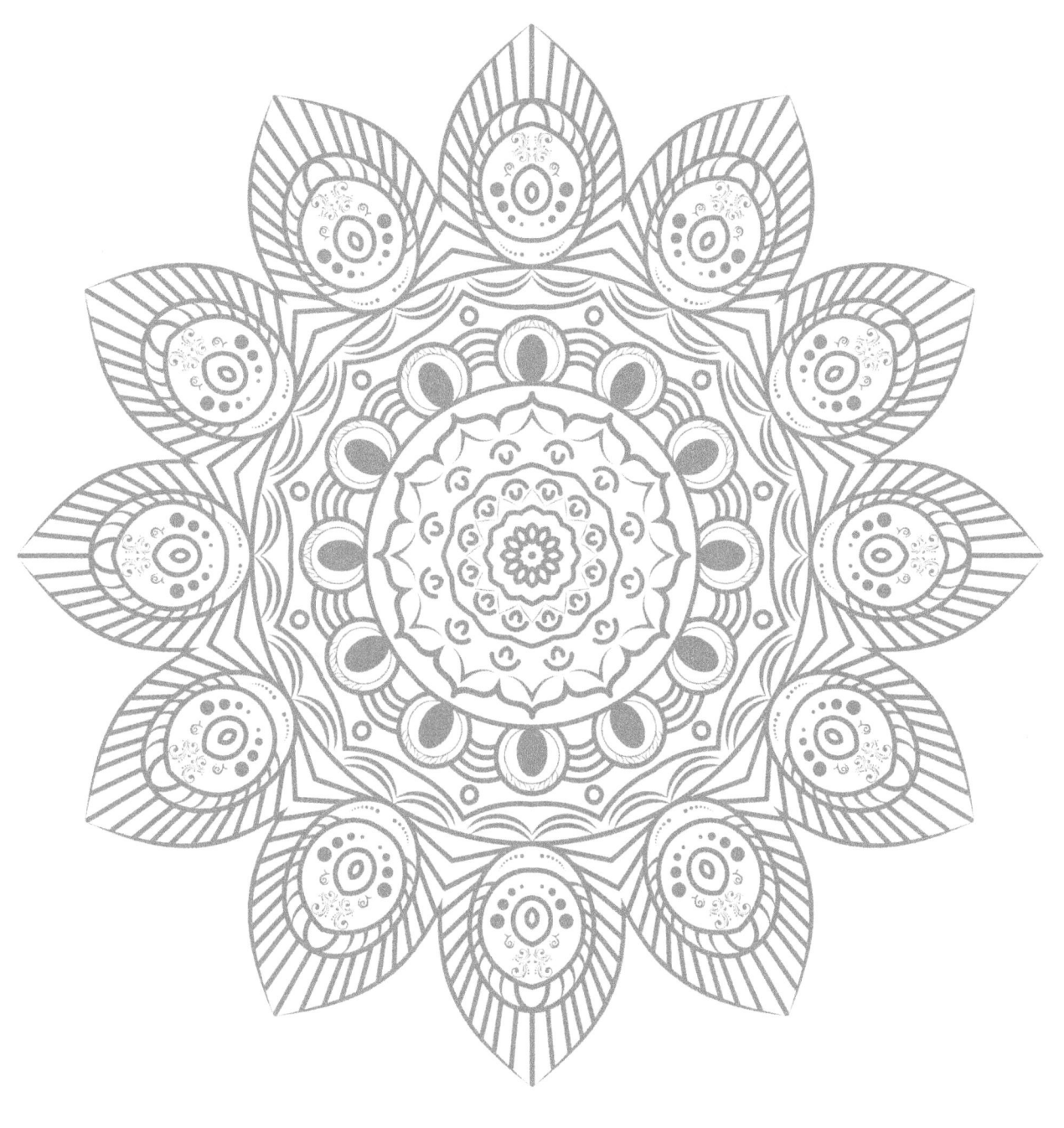

"Relax, breathe, and trust the process."

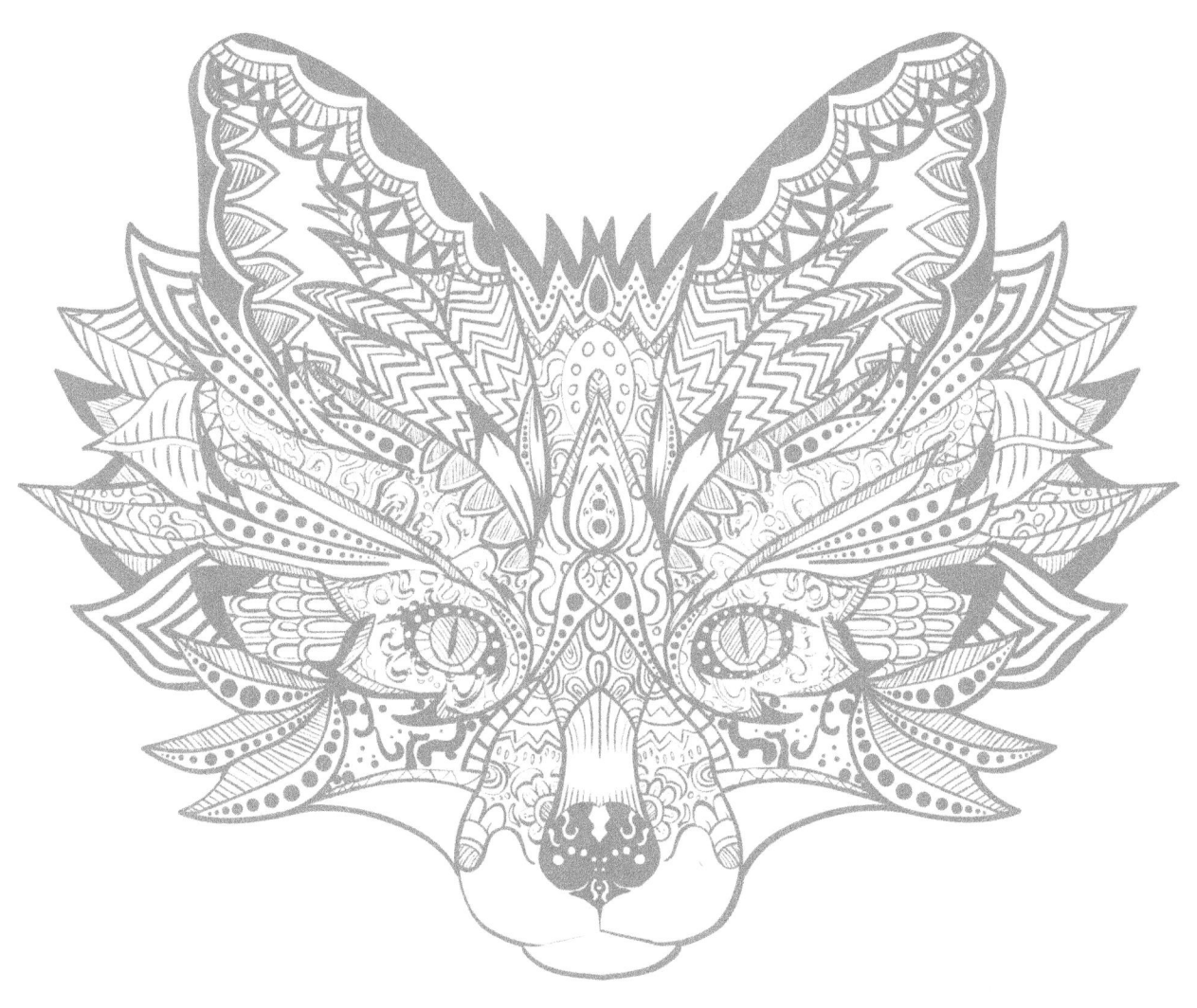

"The greatest weapon against stress is our ability to choose one thought over another."

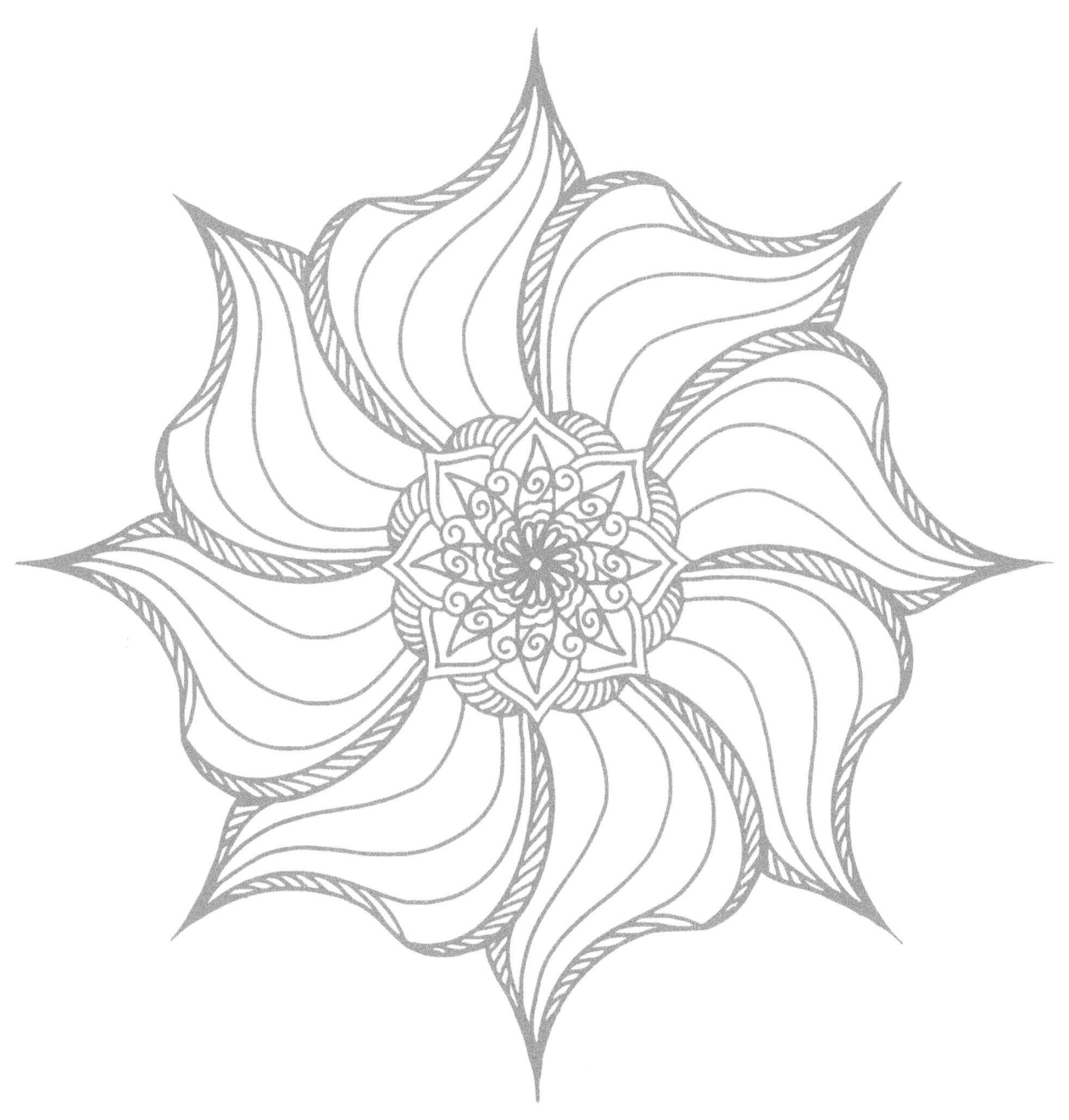

"Peace is not absence of conflict, it is the ability to handle conflict by peaceful means."

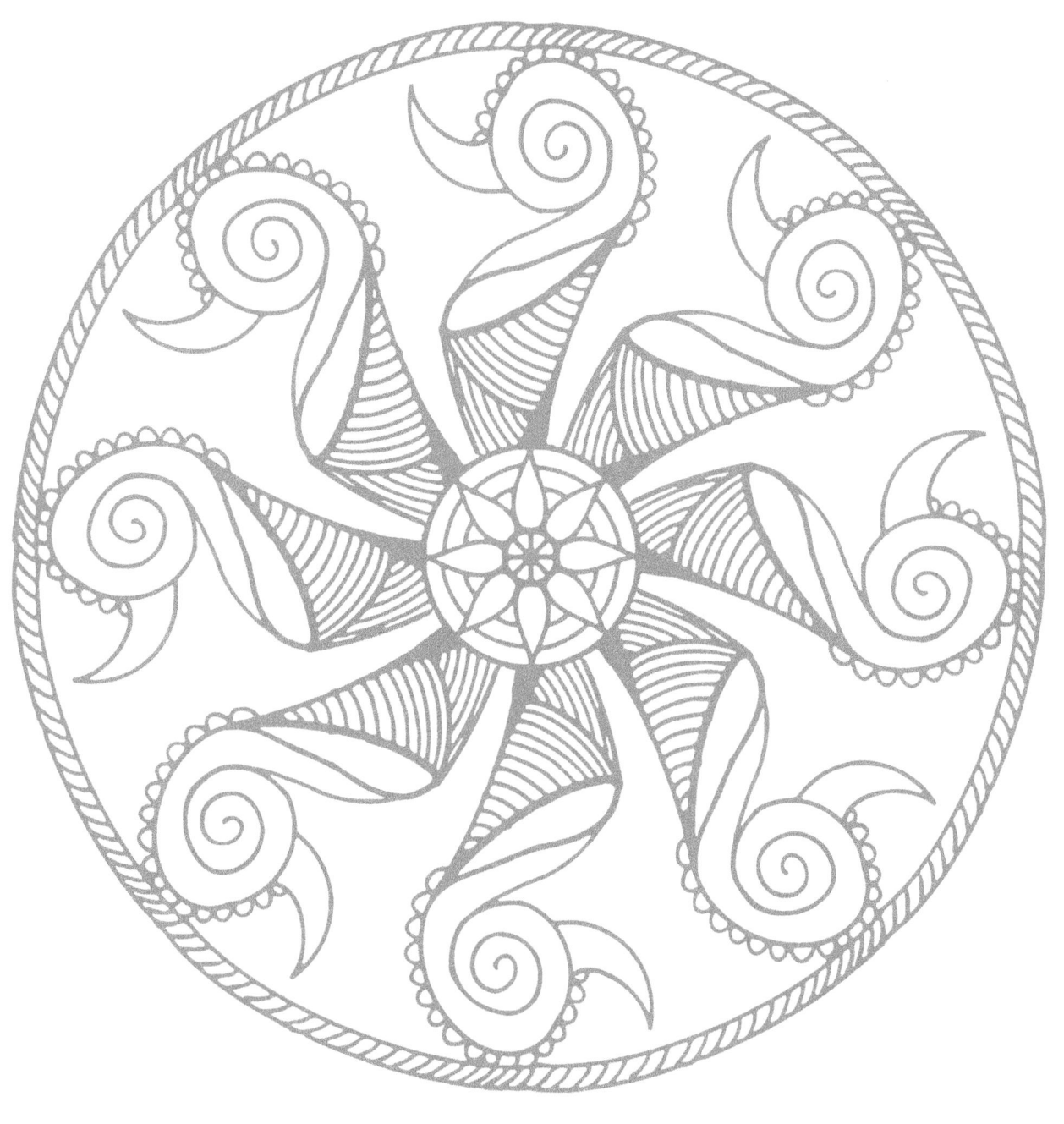

"In the midst of chaos, there
is also opportunity."

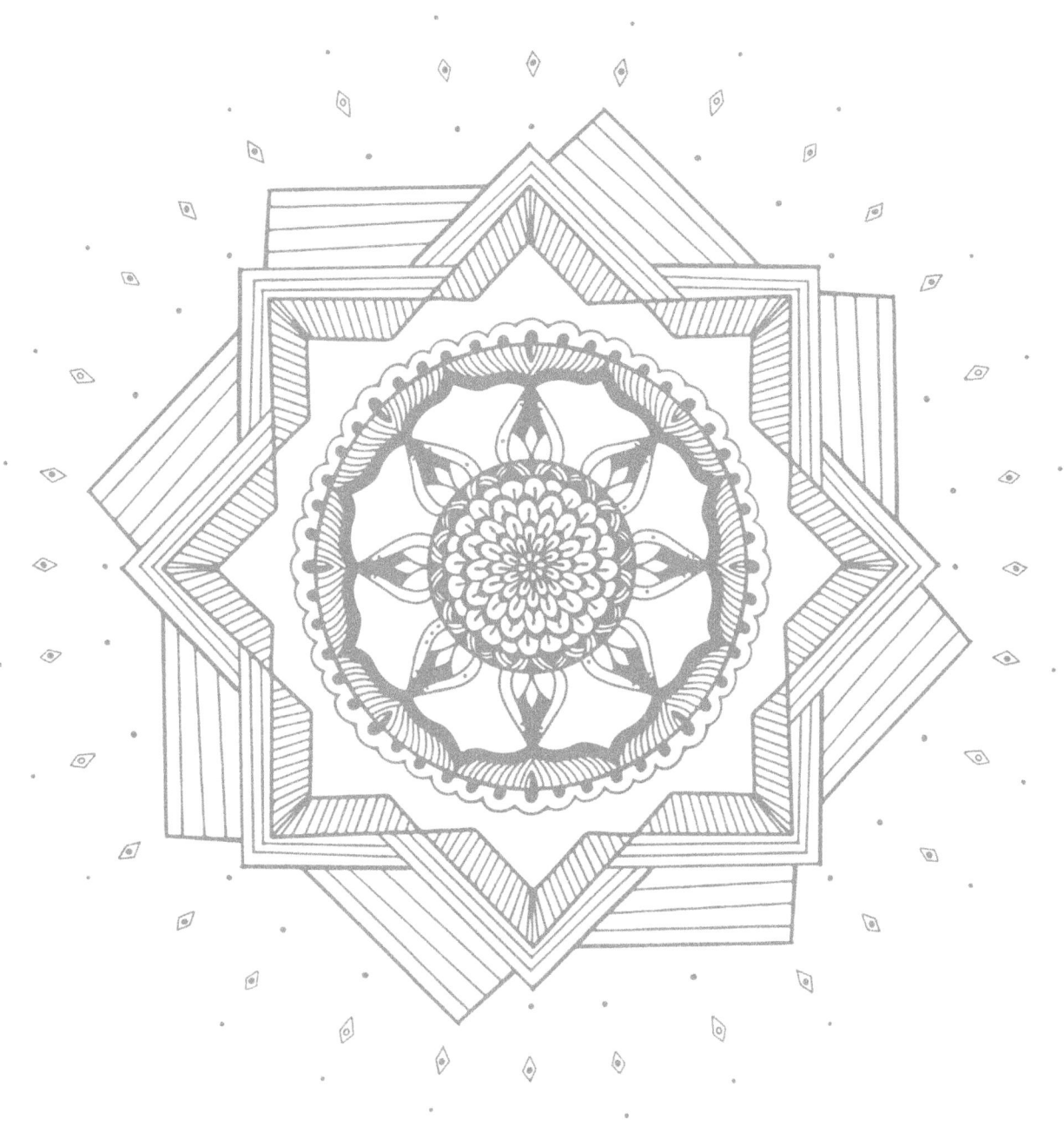

"Be still and let the peace within you guide your path."

"Do less, be more."

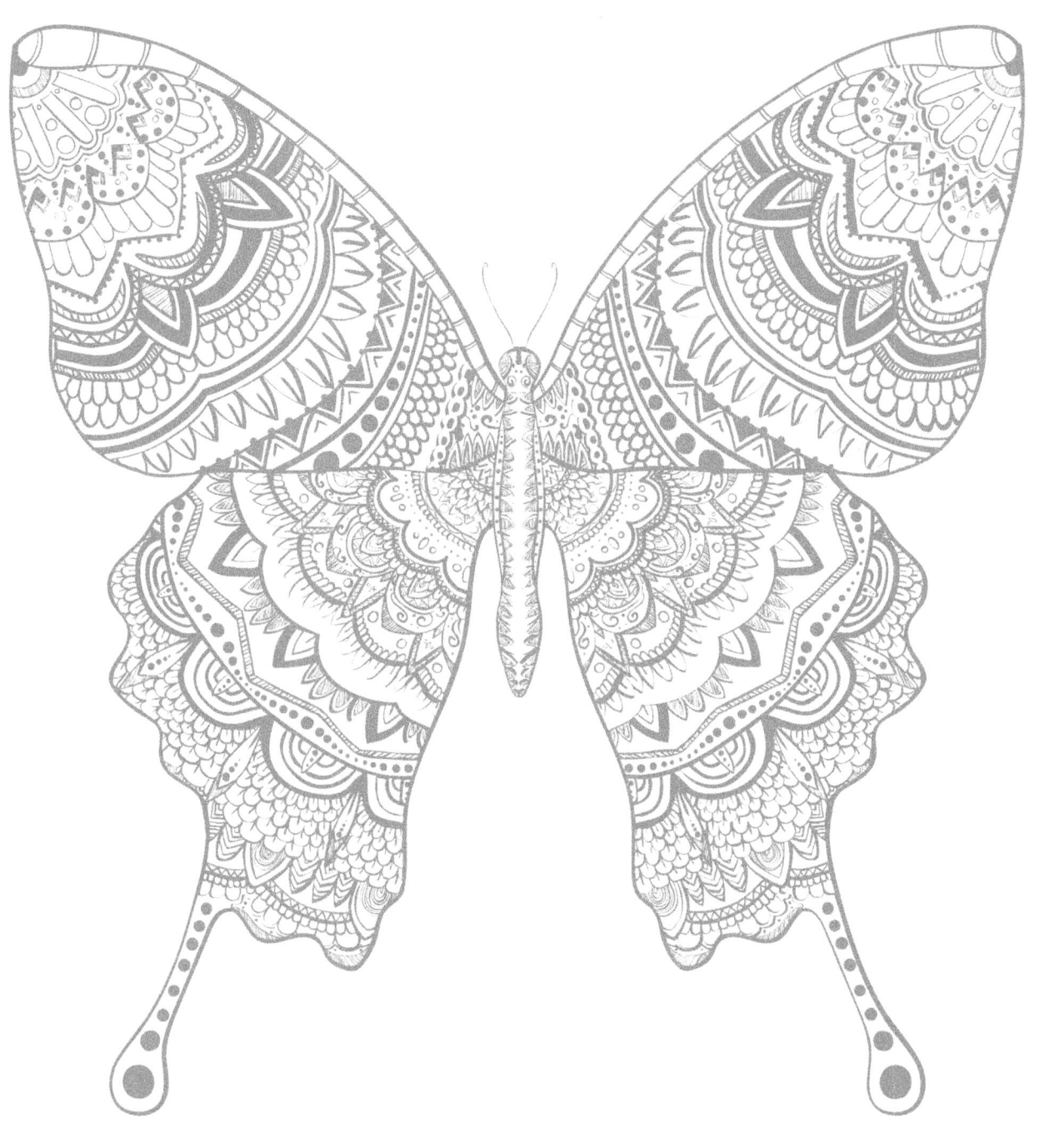

"The quieter you become,
the more you can hear."

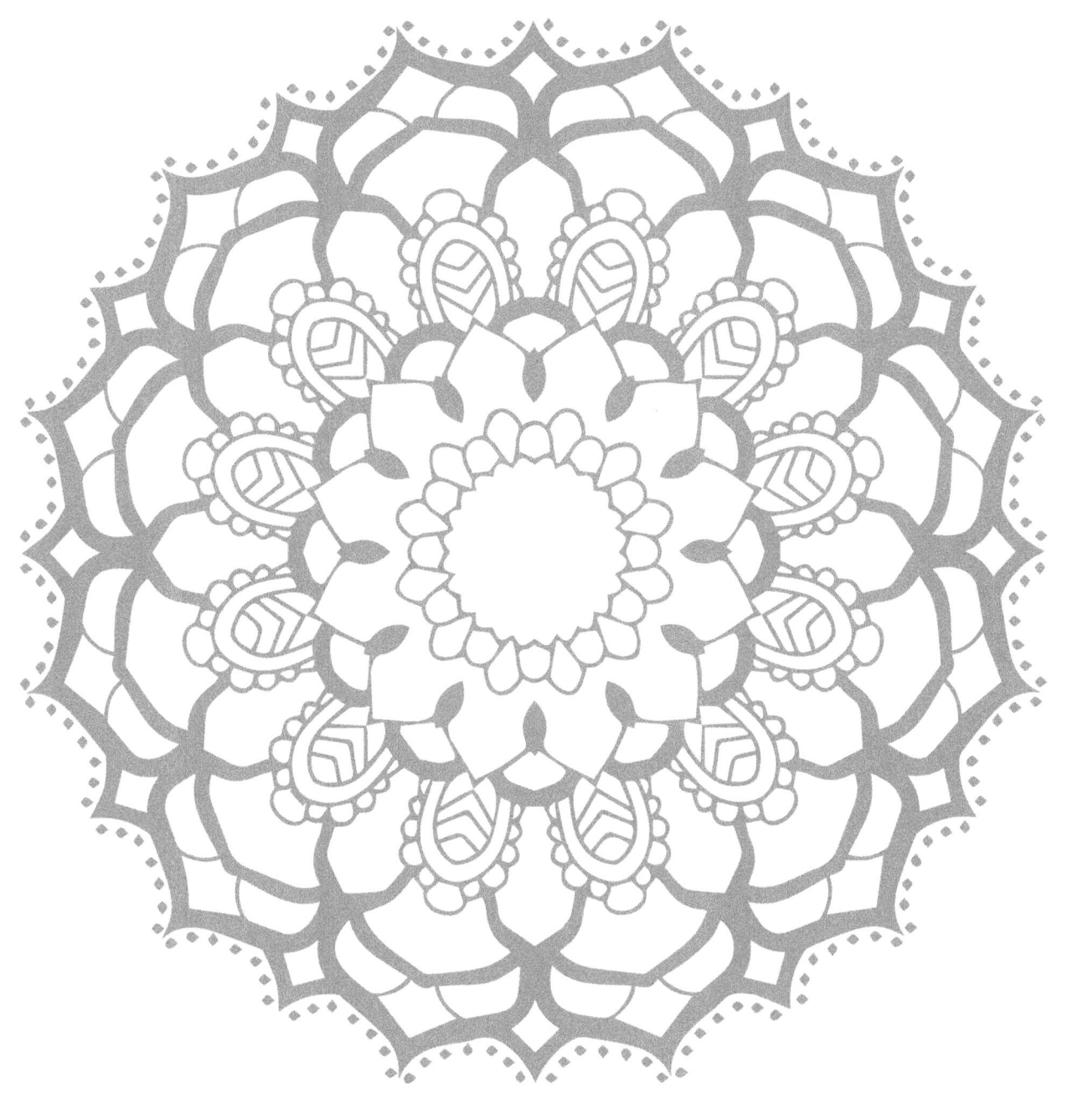

"Let go of the thoughts that don't make you strong."

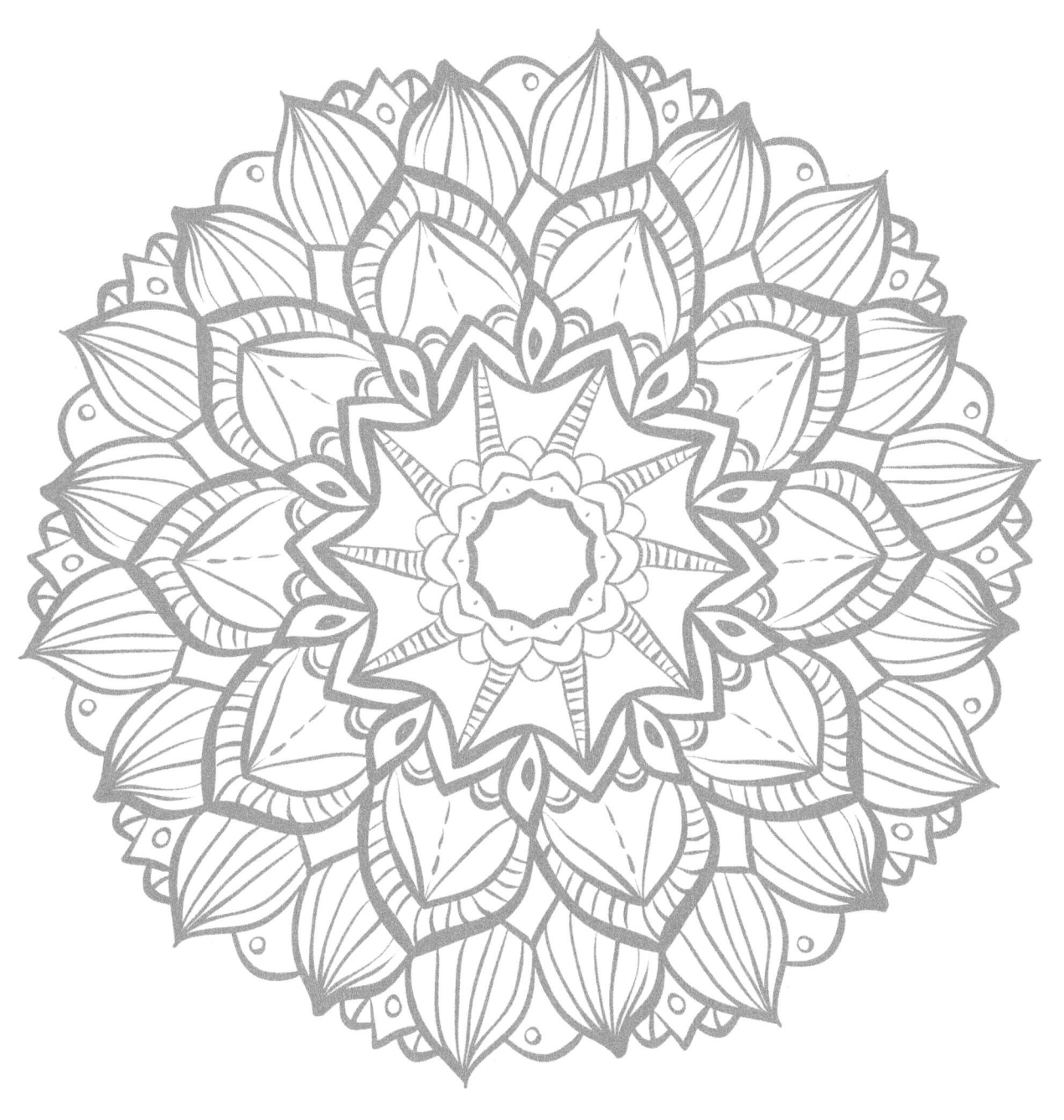

"In the world of nothingness,
hold on to peace."

"Relaxation is the key to all
that you seek."

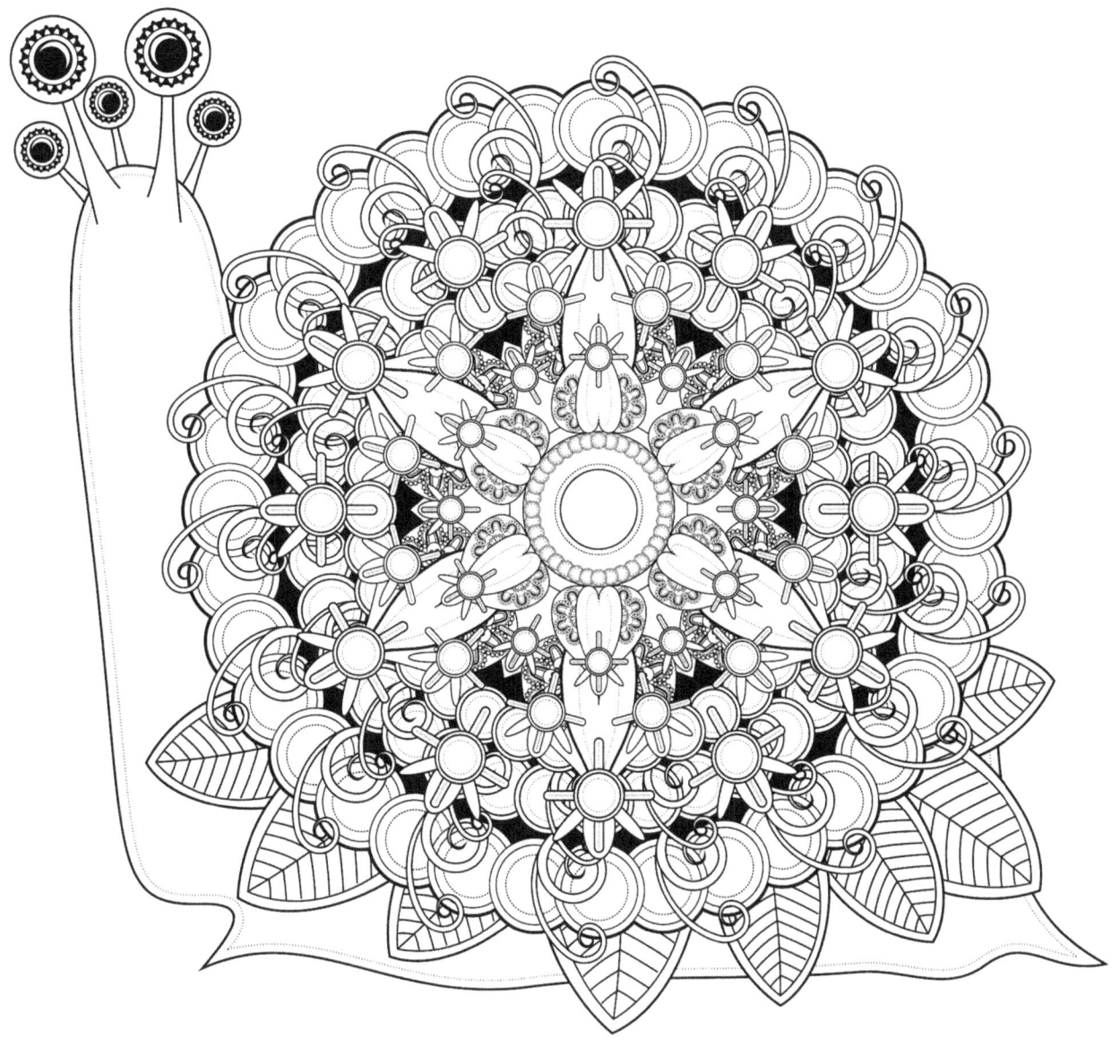

"The present moment is the only moment available to us, and it is the door to all moments."

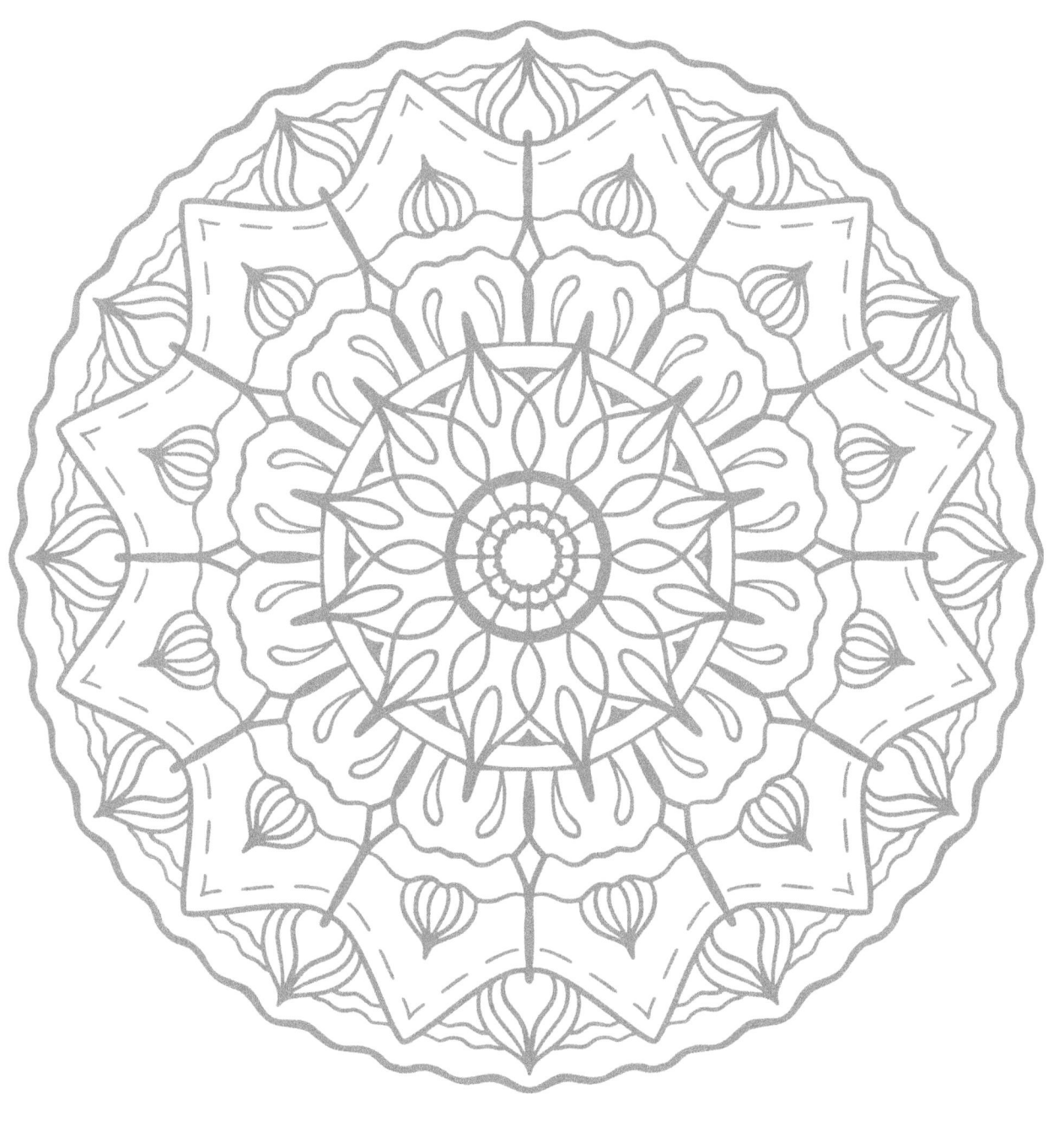

"Serenity is not freedom from the storm but peace amid the storm."

"Don't let yesterday take up
too much of today."

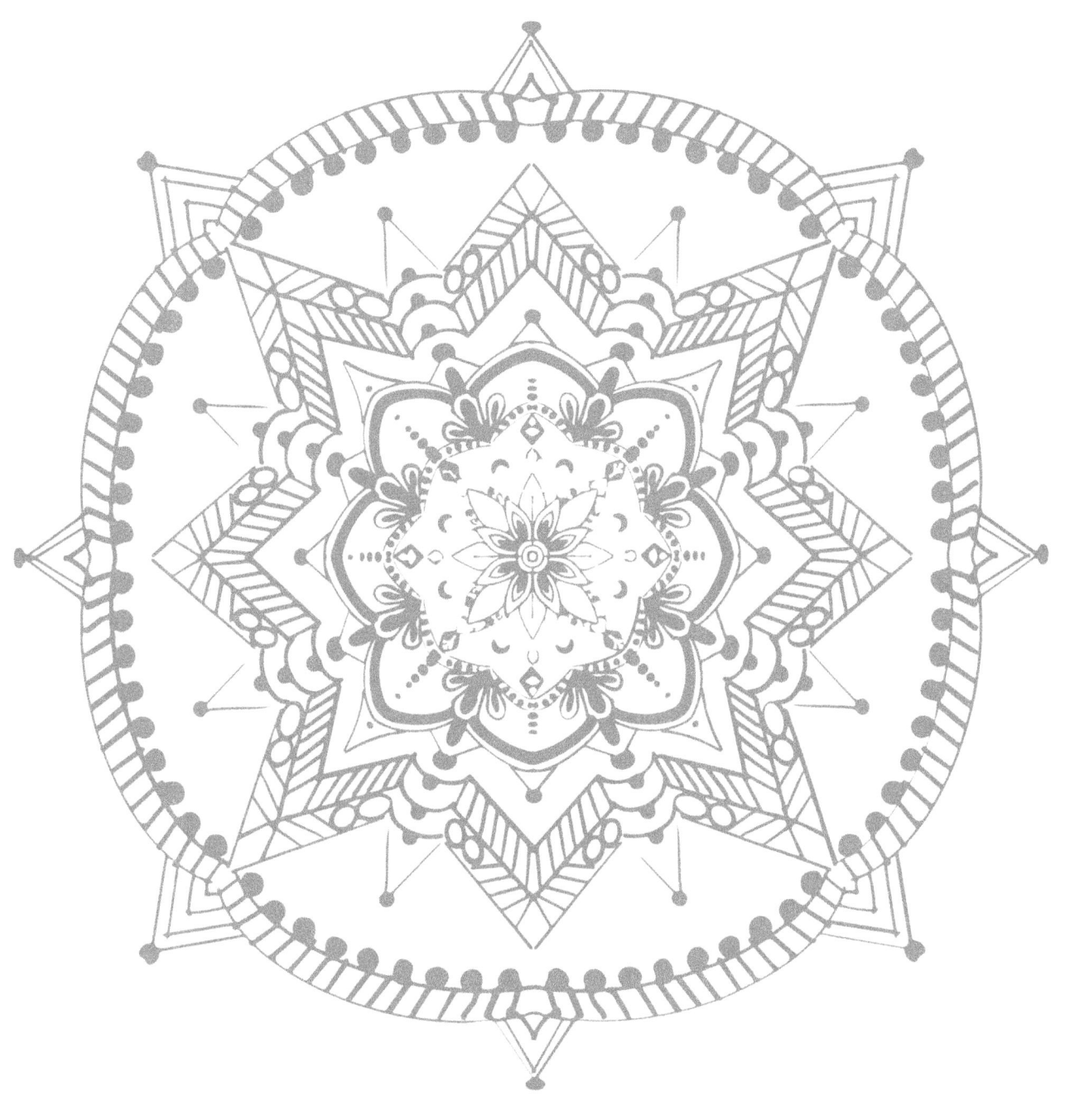

"When you realize nothing is lacking,
the whole world belongs to you."

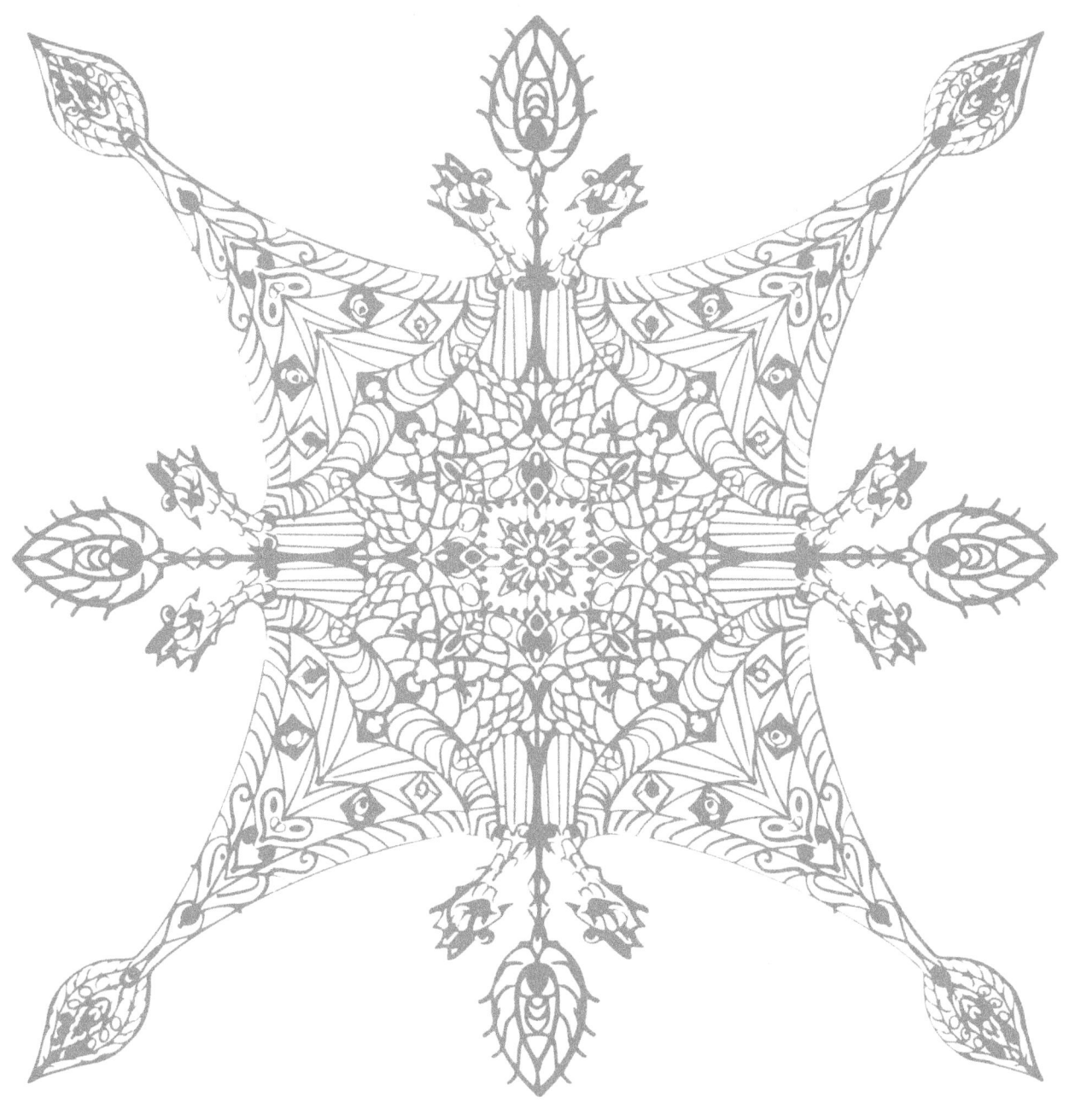

"Peace is not something you find.
It's something you create."

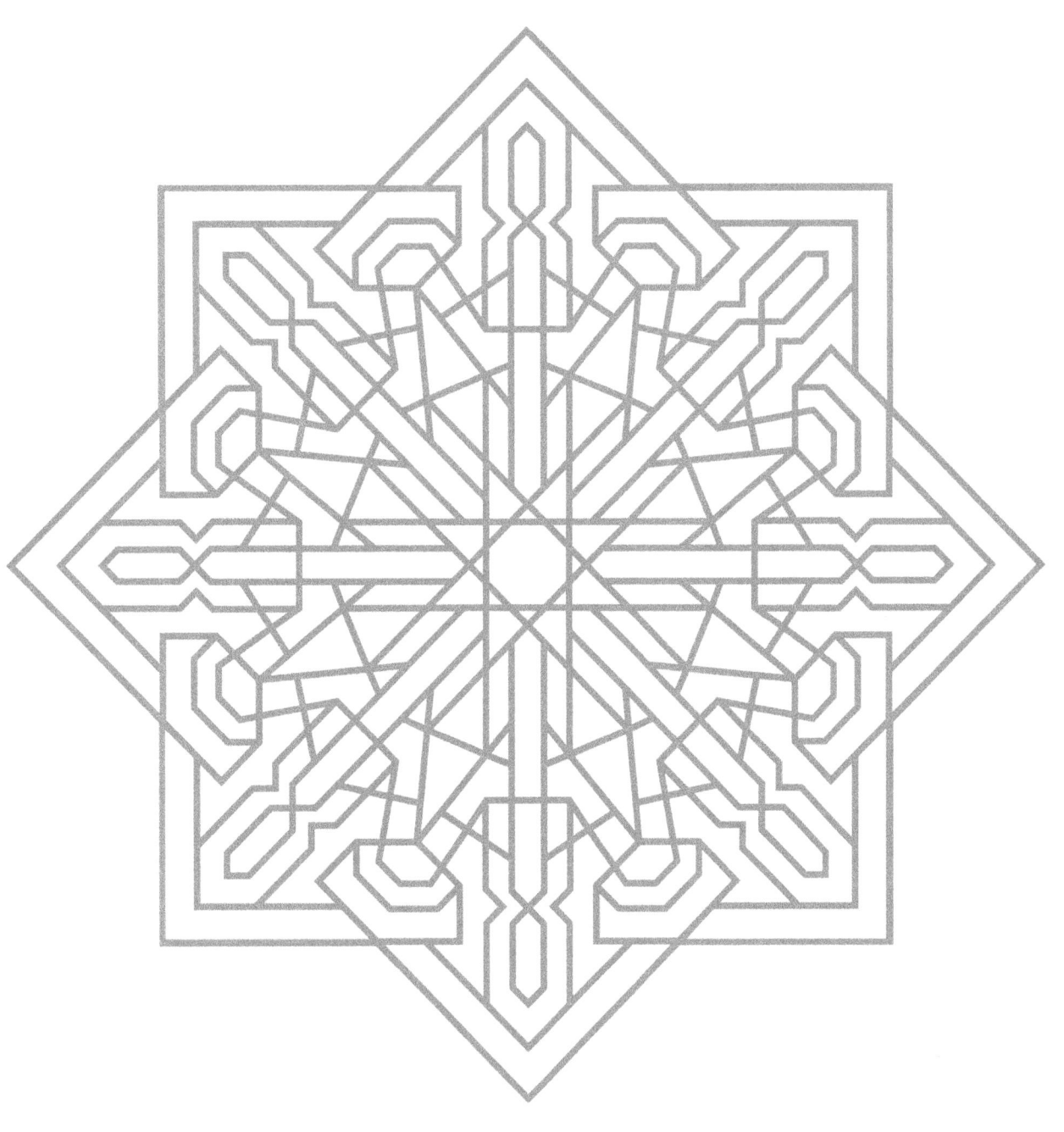

"Find your inner peace and let it radiate outward."

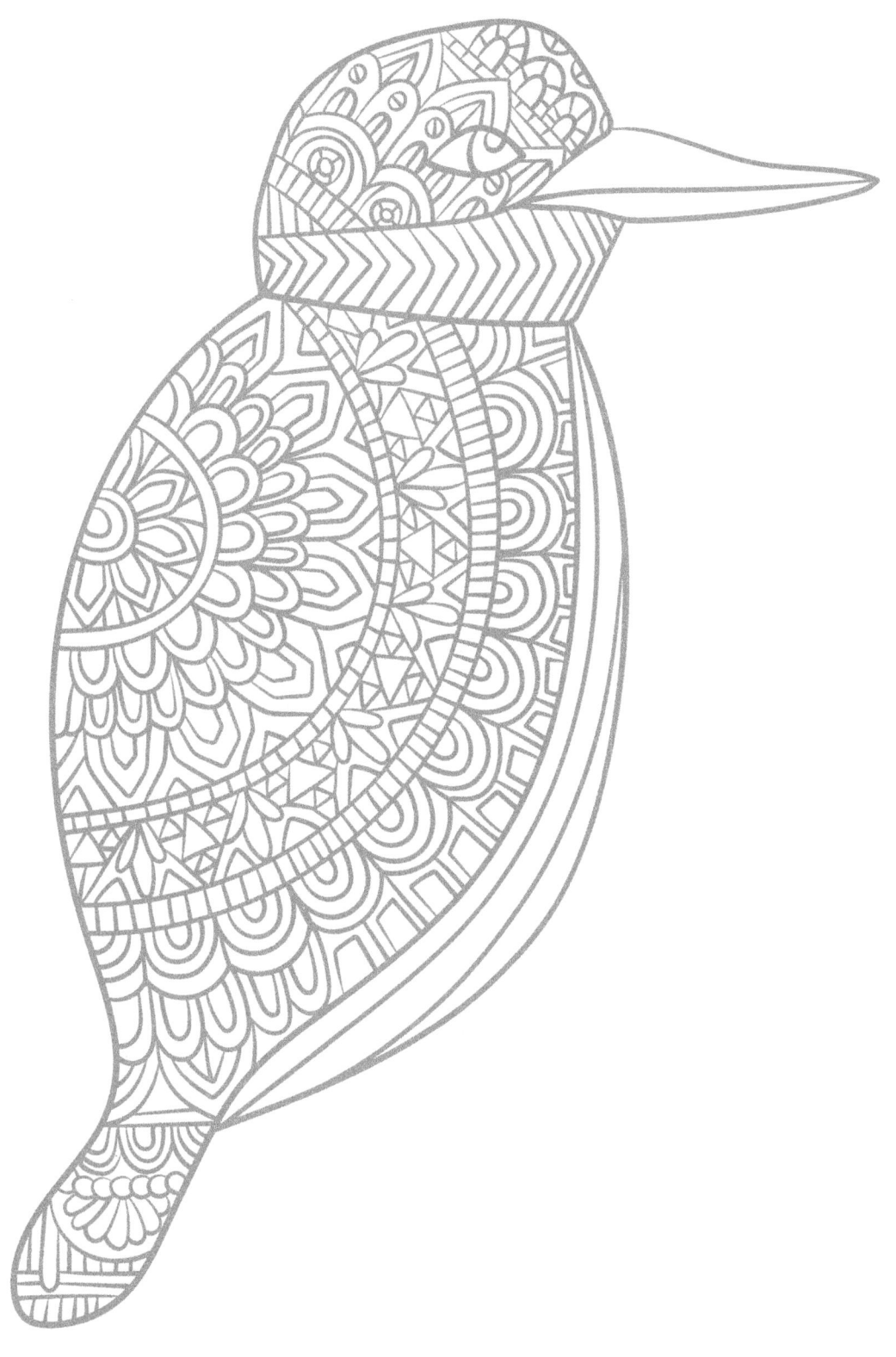

"Learn to be calm and you will always be happy."

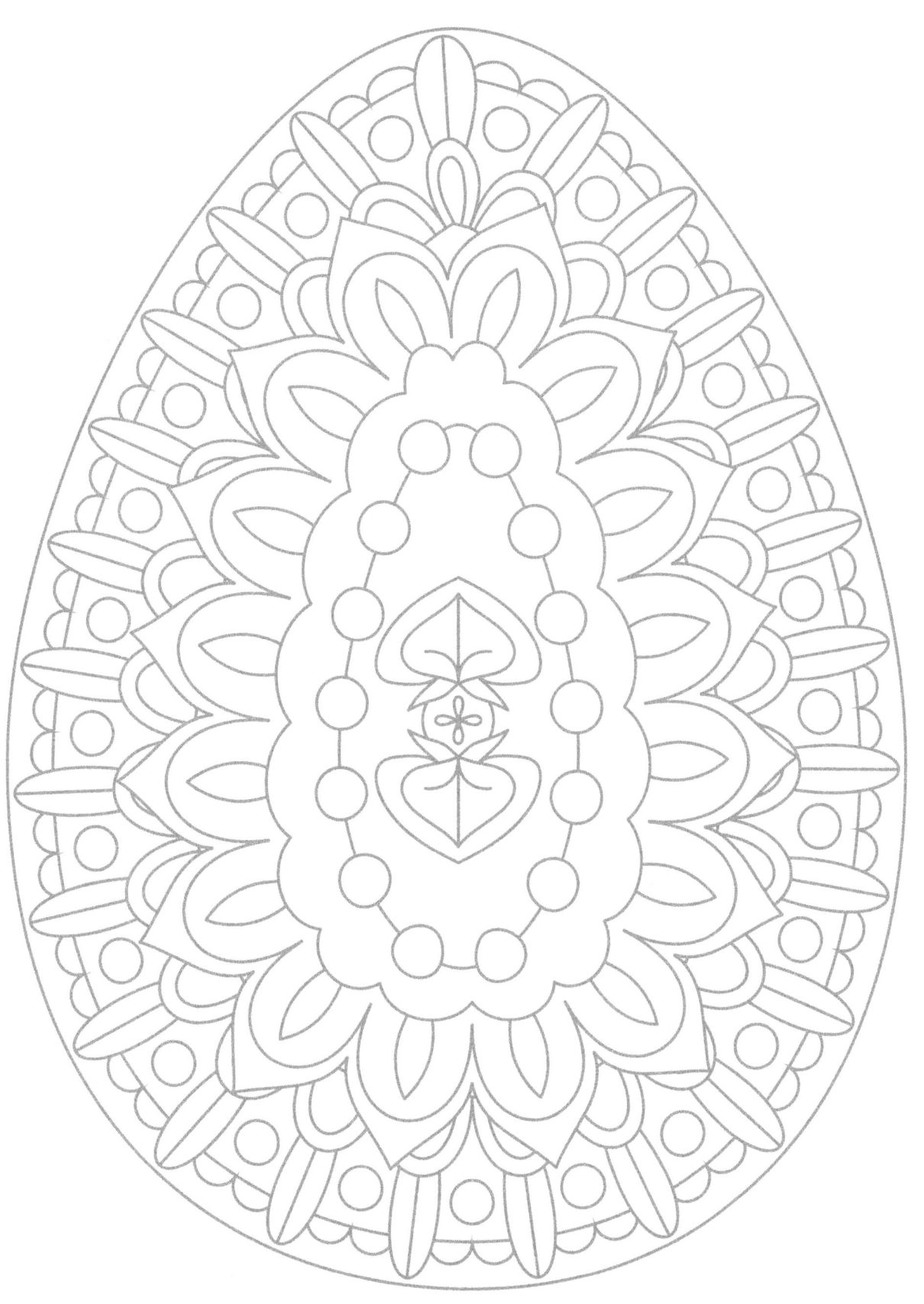

"Stillness is where creativity and solutions are found."

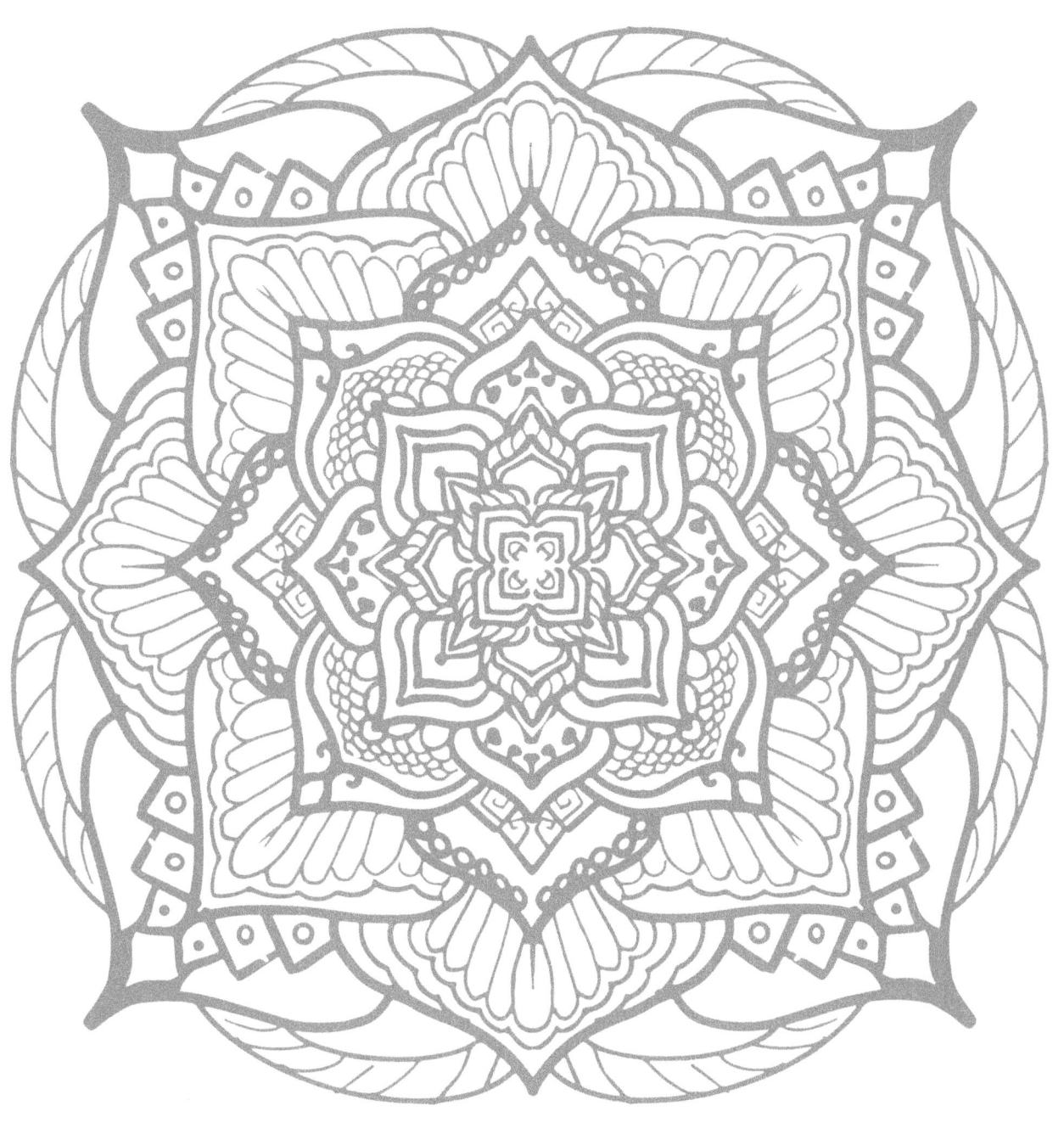

"Do not let the behavior of others
destroy your inner peace."

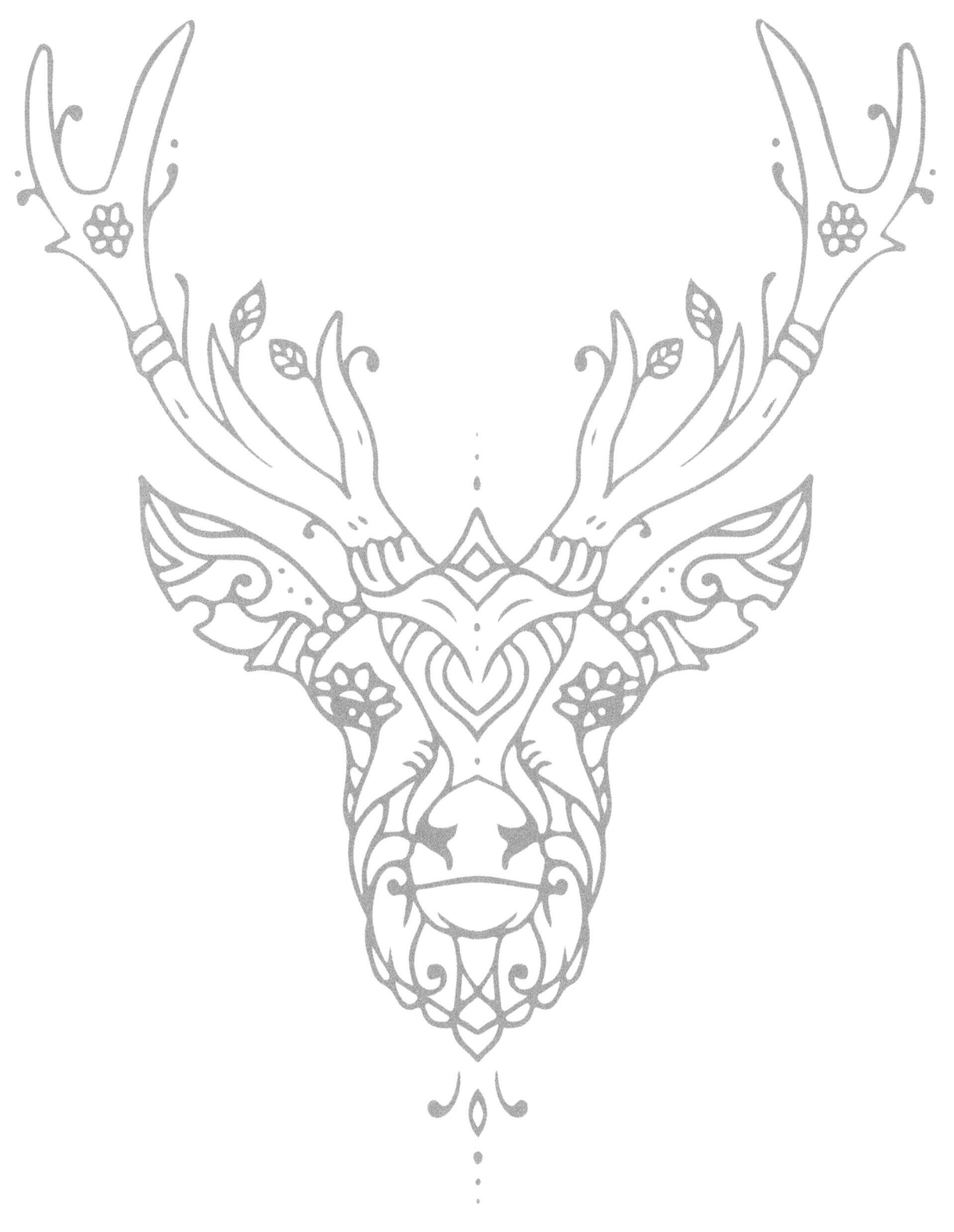

"Create a quiet space within yourself where peace and tranquility can flourish."

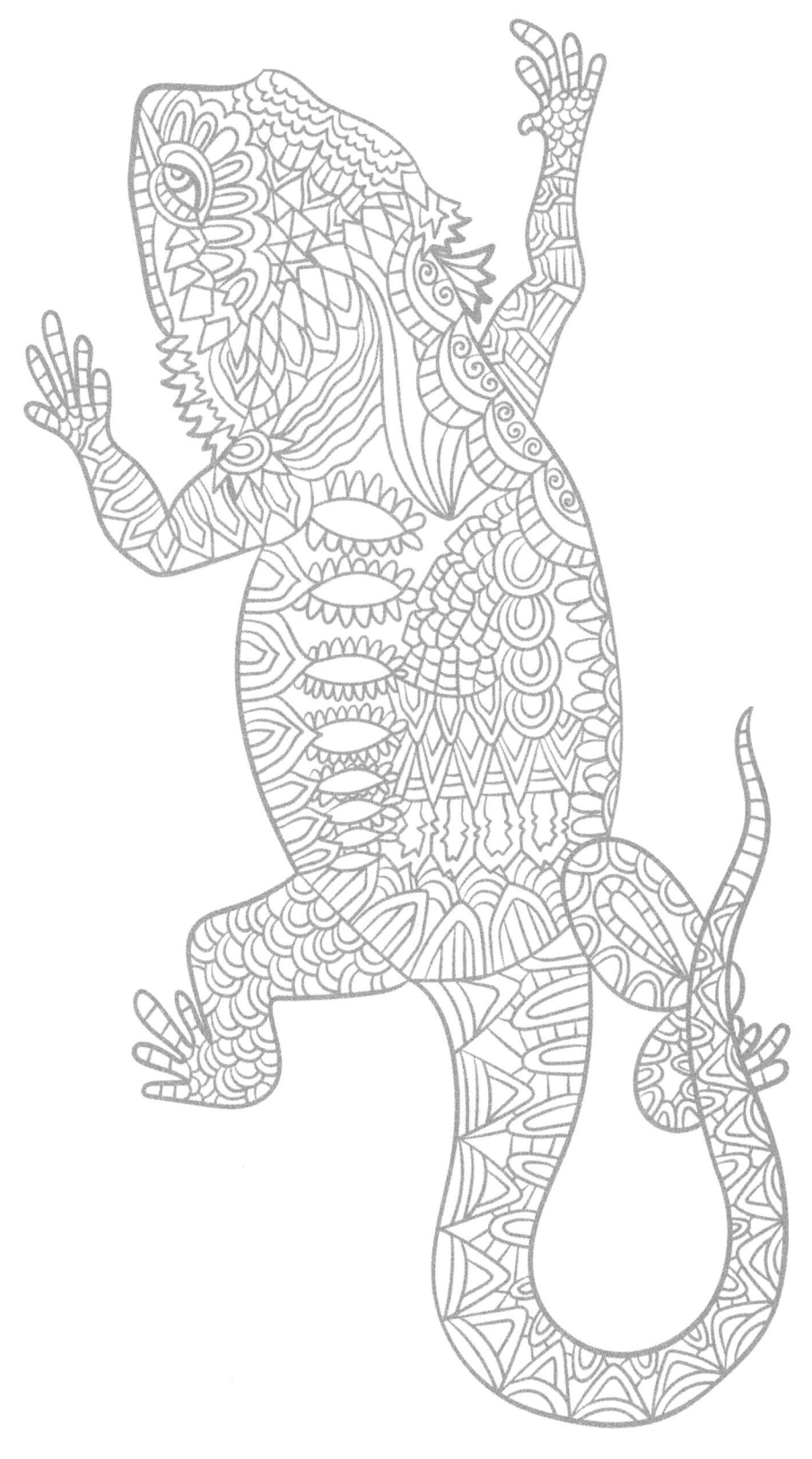

"Peace begins with a smile."

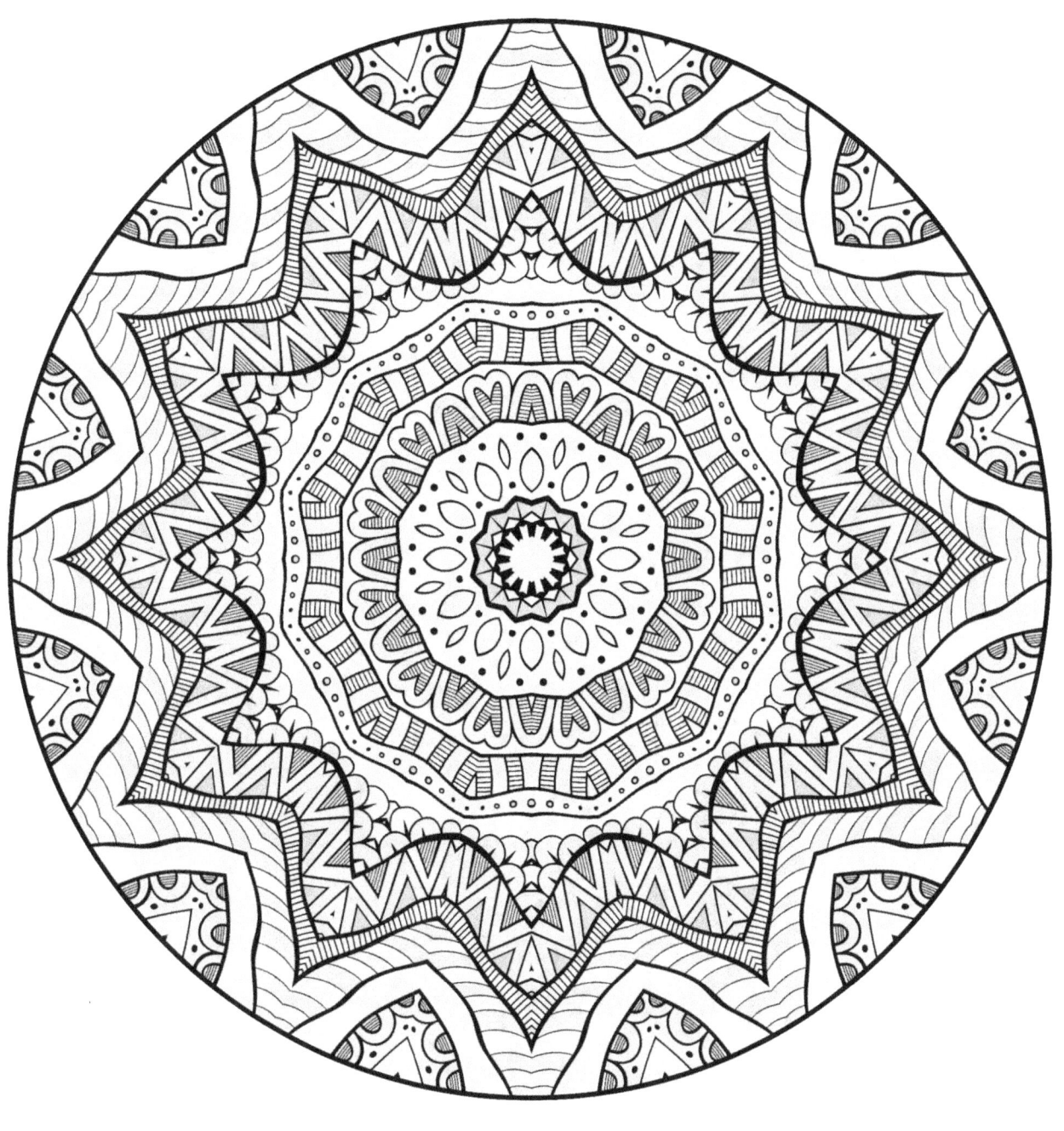

"Relaxation is the prerequisite for inner growth and transformation."

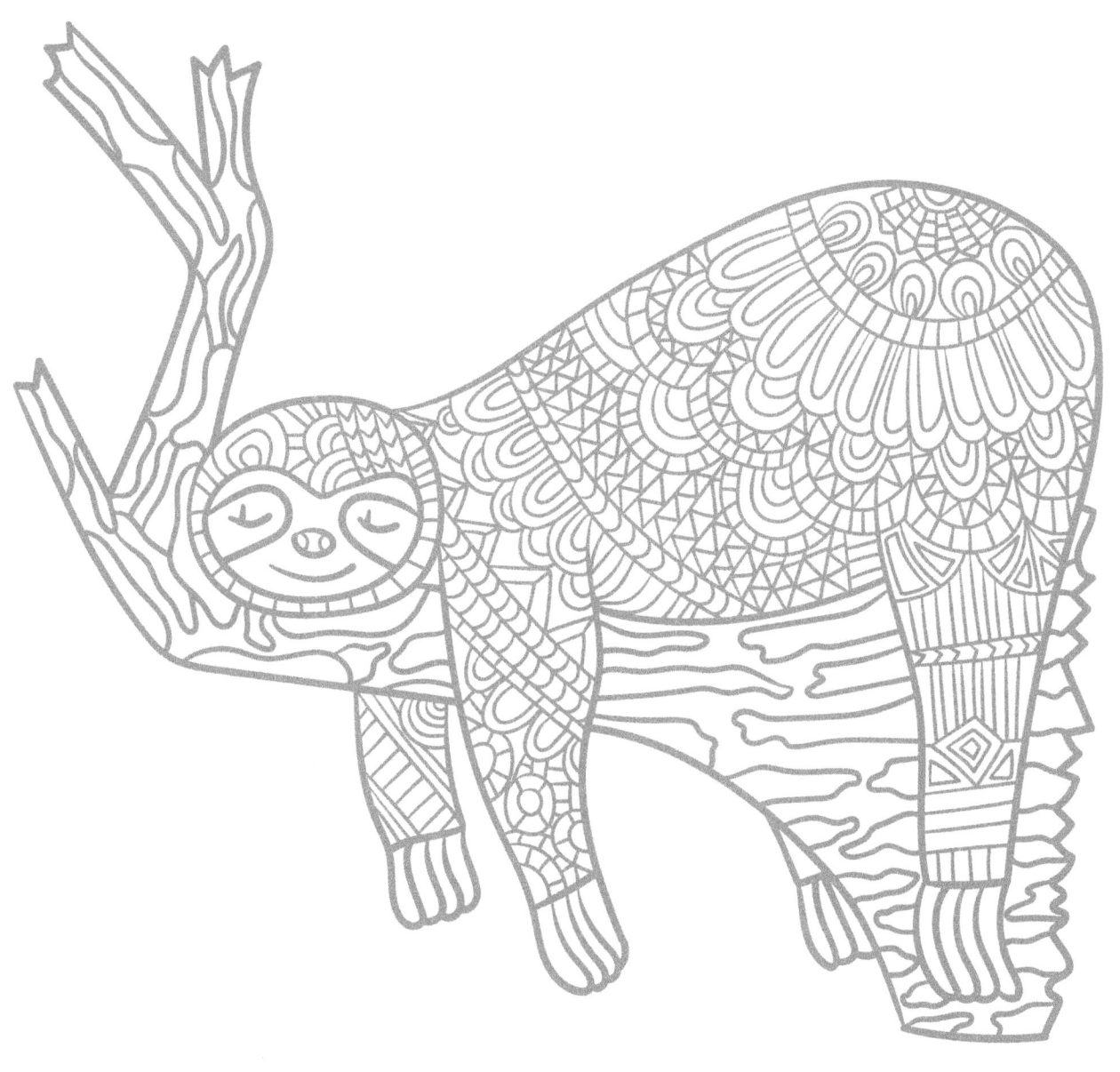

"The mind is everything.
What you think, you become."

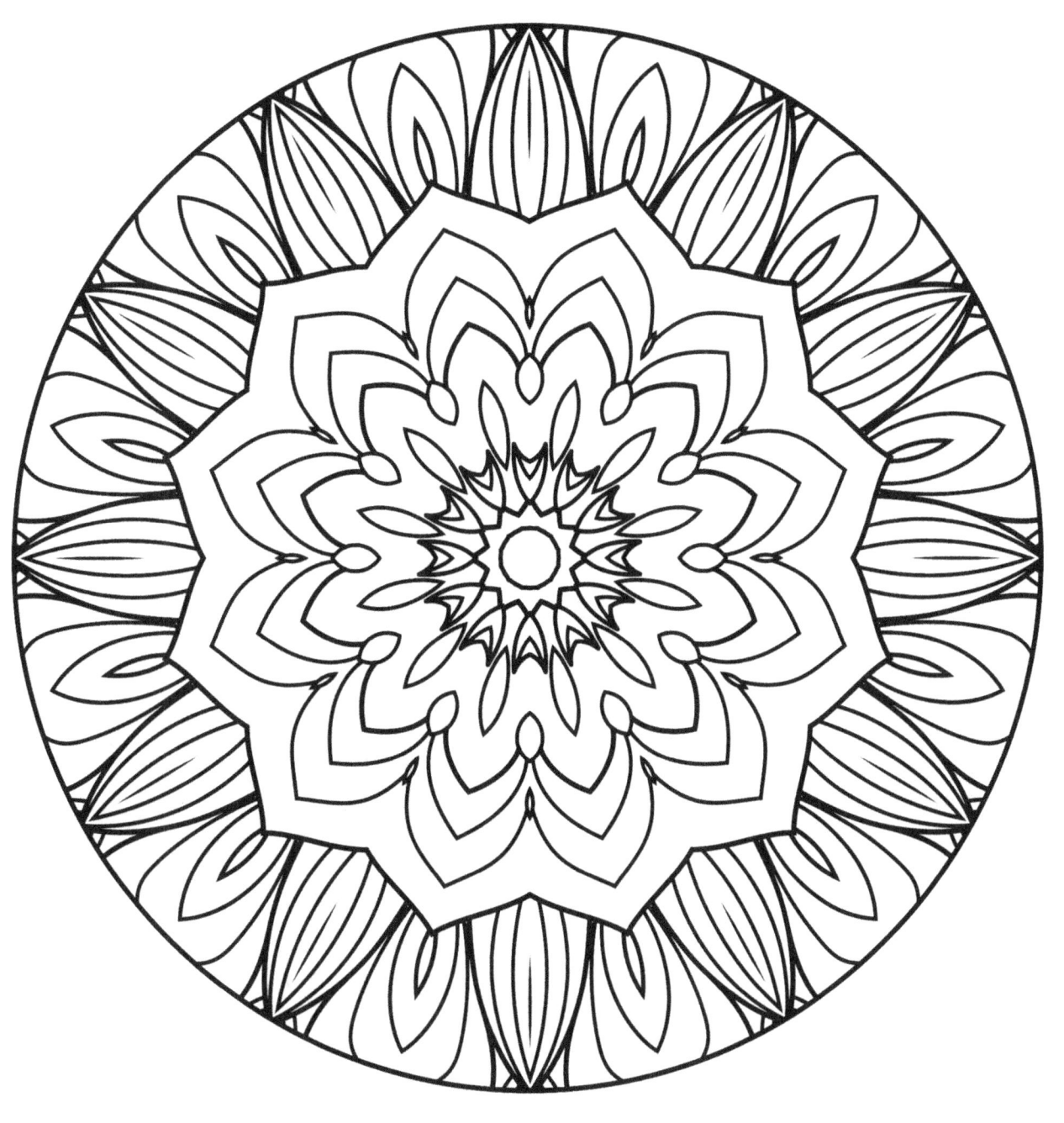

"Find joy in the present moment and peace will follow."

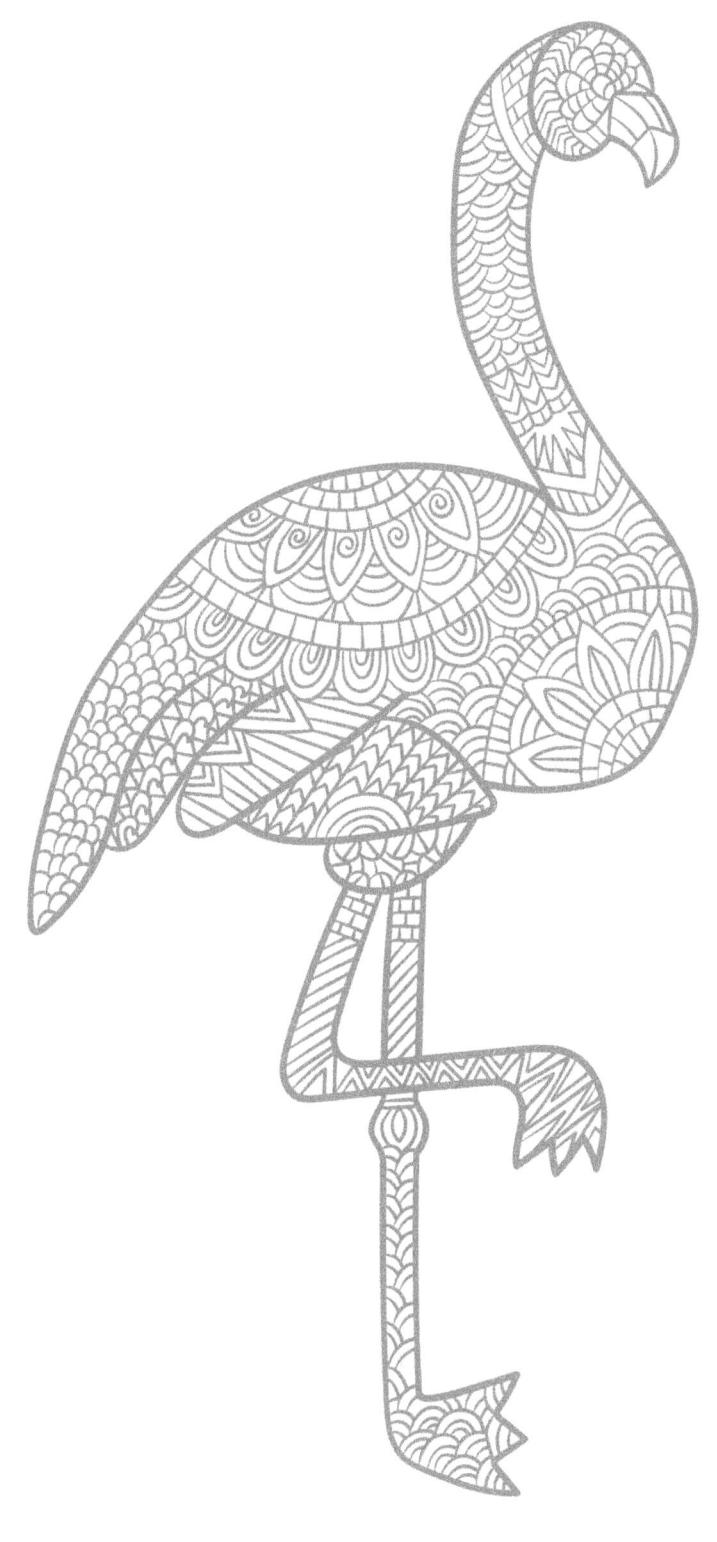

"Happiness is a state of inner peace."

"Let go of the need to control and
find peace in surrender."

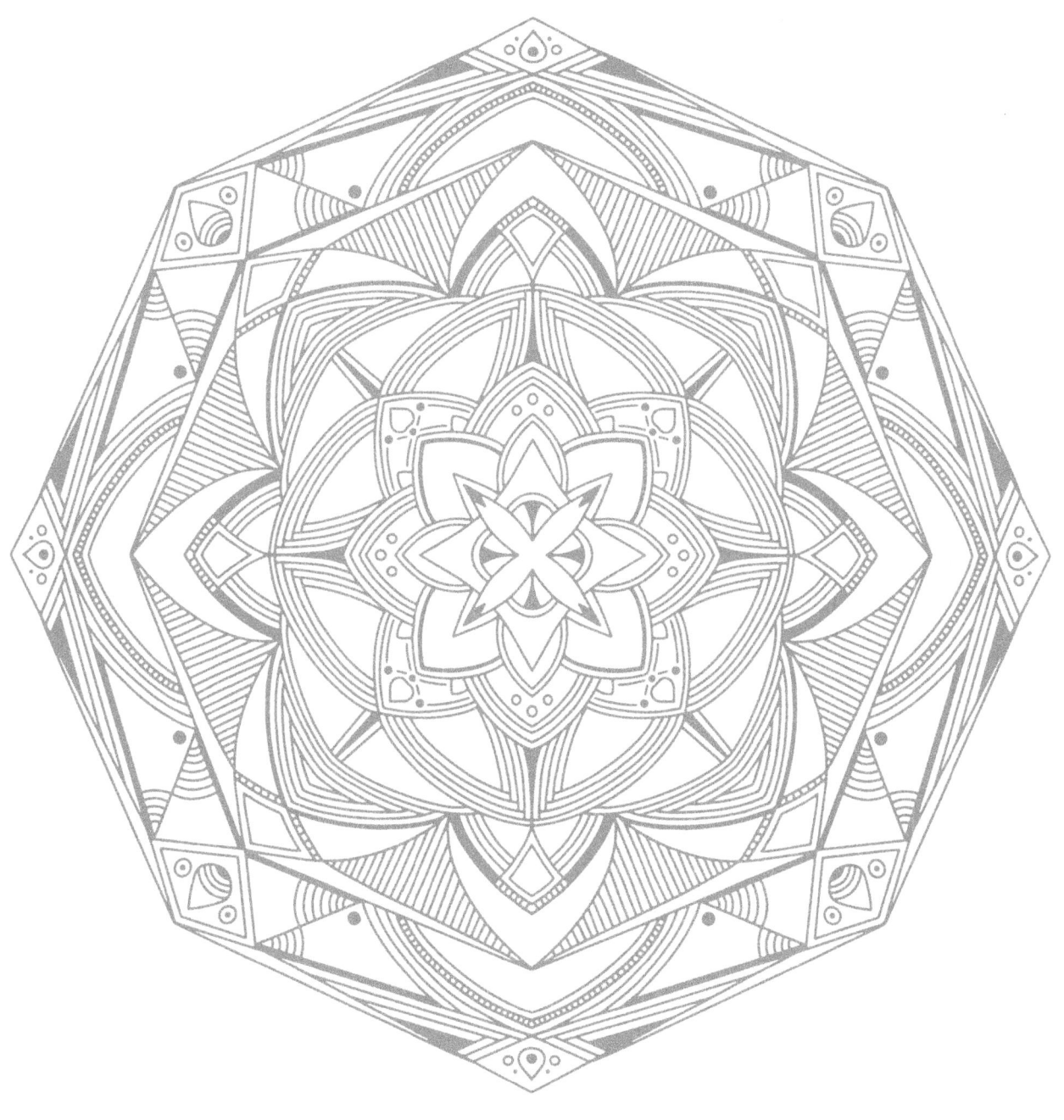

"The less you respond to negativity,
the more peaceful your life becomes."

"Don't hurry, don't worry. You're only here for a short visit. So don't forget to stop and smell the roses."

"Let the waves of relaxation wash over your body and mind."

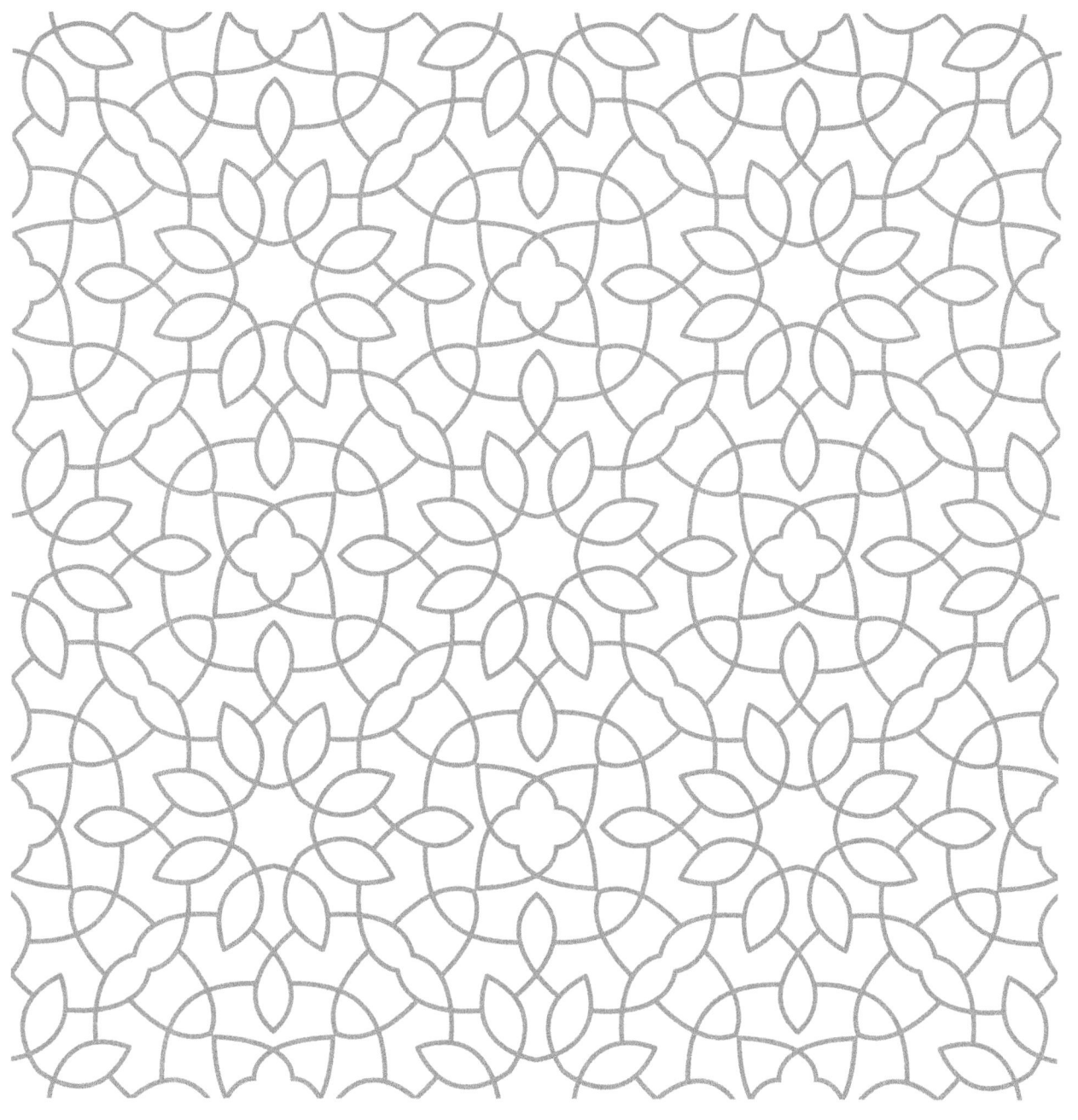

"Peace begins with a mindful breath."